THE PRISON OF LOVE

MYSTICISM AND MODERN MAN

The Prison of Love

Selections from St. Teresa of Avila

edited by Catharine Hughes

Sheed & Ward · New York

The quotations are from *The Complete Works of St. Teresa,* translated and edited by E. Allison Peers, 3 vols. (New York: Sheed and Ward, 1950); *Life of Saint Teresa of Jesus, written by herself,* translated by David Lewis (London: Burns, Oates, 1870); and *Letters of St. Teresa,* translated by the Benedictines of Stanbrook (London: Thomas Baker).

Library of Congress Cataloging in Publication Data

Teresa, Saint, 1515-1582.
　The prison of love.

　(Mysticism and modern man)
　1.　Catholic Church—Collected works.　2.　Theology—Collected works—16th century.　3.　Mysticism—Collected works.　I.　Hughes, Catharine, 1935-　　ed. II.　Title.
BX890.T39 1972　　201'.1　　72-6606
ISBN 0-8362-0503-0

Perhaps we do not know what love is . . .

Then He said: "Ah, My daughter, they are few who love Me in truth; for if men loved Me, I should not hide My secrets from them. Knowest thou what it is to love Me in truth? It is to admit everything to be a lie which is not pleasing unto Me."

We creatures go about like silly little shepherd boys, thinking we are learning to know something of Thee when the very most we can know amounts to nothing at all, for even in ourselves there are deep secrets which we cannot fathom.

2

How long will it be . . . before we imitate this great God in any way?

3

4

Will pleasures and pastimes lead us to the fruition of what He won for us at the cost of so much blood? . . . Do we think that by accepting vain honors we shall be following Him Who was despised so that we might reign forever?

If we fill the palace with vulgar people and all kinds of junk, how can the Lord and His Court occupy it?

It has sometimes seemed to me . . . that the devils behave as though they were playing ball with the soul, so incapable is it of freeing itself from their power. . . . Its eyes seem to be almost blindfolded: it is like someone who has gone along a particular road again and again, so that, even if it is night and quite dark, he knows by instinct which comes from experience where he is likely to stumble, for he has seen the road by day and is therefore on his guard against the danger. Just so the soul, in avoiding giving offense to God, seems to be walking by habit. . . . The Lord has it in His keeping.

The Creator must be sought through
the creatures.

We shall never succeed in knowing ourselves unless we seek to know God: let us think of His greatness and then come back to our own baseness; by looking at His purity we shall see our foulness; by meditating upon His humility, we shall see how far we are from being humble.

Remember how many are now in the depths
who were once on the heights.

10

There is no happiness that is secure and nothing that does not change. . . . If only we thought carefully about the things of life, we should each find by experience how little either of happiness or of unhappiness there is to be got from it!

11

On earth we are but pilgrims.

I live, yet no true life I know,
And, living thus expectantly,
I die because I do not die.

Since this new death-in-life I've known,
Estrang'd from self my life has been,
For now I live a life unseen:
The Lord has claim'd me as His own.
My heart I gave Him for His throne,
Whereon he wrote indelibly:
"I die because I do not die."

Within this prison-house divine,
Prison of love whereby I live,
My God Himself to me doth give,
And liberate this heart of mine.
And, as with love I yearn and pine,
With God my prisoner, I sigh:
"I die because I do not die."

13

How tedious is this life below,
This exile, with its griefs and pains,
This dungeon and these cruel chains
In which the soul is forced to go!
Straining to leave this life of woe,
With anguish sharp and deep I cry:
"I die because I do not die."

16

How bitter our existence ere
We come at last the Lord to meet!
For, though the soul finds loving sweet,
The waiting-time is hard to bear.
Oh, from this leaden weight of care,
My God, relieve me speedily,
Who die because I do not die.

17

Consider, life, love's potency,
And cease to cause me grief and pain.
Reflect, I beg, that, thee to gain,
I first must lose thee utterly.
Then, death, come pleasantly to me.
Come softly: undismay'd am I
Who die because I do not die.

It is no small pity, and should cause us no little shame, that, through our own fault, we do not understand ourselves or know who we are. . . . All our interest is centered in the rough setting of the diamond and in the outer wall of the castle—in these bodies of ours.

19

What power is that of a soul brought hither by the Lord, which can look upon everything without being ensnared by it! How ashamed it is of the time when it was attached to everything! How amazed it is at its blindness!

I began to think of the soul as if it were a castle made of a single diamond or of very clear crystal, in which there are many rooms, just as in Heaven there are many mansions. . . . There is no point in our fatiguing ourselves by attempting to comprehend the beauty of this castle; for the very fact that His Majesty says it is made in His image means that we can hardly form any conception of the soul's great dignity and beauty.

20

The Lord does not look so much at the magnitude of anything we do as at the love with which we do it.

In every little thing created by God there is more than we realize, even in so small a thing as a tiny ant.

23

24

We cannot be sure if we are loving God, although we may have good reasons for believing that we are, but we can know quite well if we are loving our neighbor.

Do you think that such persons will love none and delight in none save in God? No; they will love others much more than they did, with a more genuine love, with greater passion and with a love which brings more profit; that, in a word, is what love really is. And such souls are always much fonder of giving than of receiving, even in their relations with the Creator himself. This, I say, merits the name of love, which name has been usurped from it by those other base affections.

26

Do not be in a hurry for enjoyment; it is for mercenaries to claim their pay at the end of the day.

27

28

Any unrest and any strife can be borne if we find peace where we live; but if we would have rest from the thousand trials which afflict us in the world and the Lord is pleased to prepare such rest for us, and yet the cause of the trouble is in ourselves, the result cannot but be very painful, indeed almost unbearable.

O, Lord, how little do we Christians know Thee!
What will that day be like when Thou comest
to judge us?

Little honor
is ever done
to the poor.

31

I have never been curious about things, and I do not care to know more than I do. What I have learned, without seeking to learn . . . has been a great trouble to me, though it has been the means, I believe, which Our Lord made use of to save me.

Let nothing disturb thee;
Let nothing dismay thee:
All things pass;
God never changes.
Patience attains
All that it strives for.
He who has God
Finds He lacks nothing:
God alone suffices.

33

34

O Loveliness, that dost exceed
All other loveliness we know,
Thou woundest not, yet pain'st indeed
And painlessly the soul is freed
From love of creatures here below.

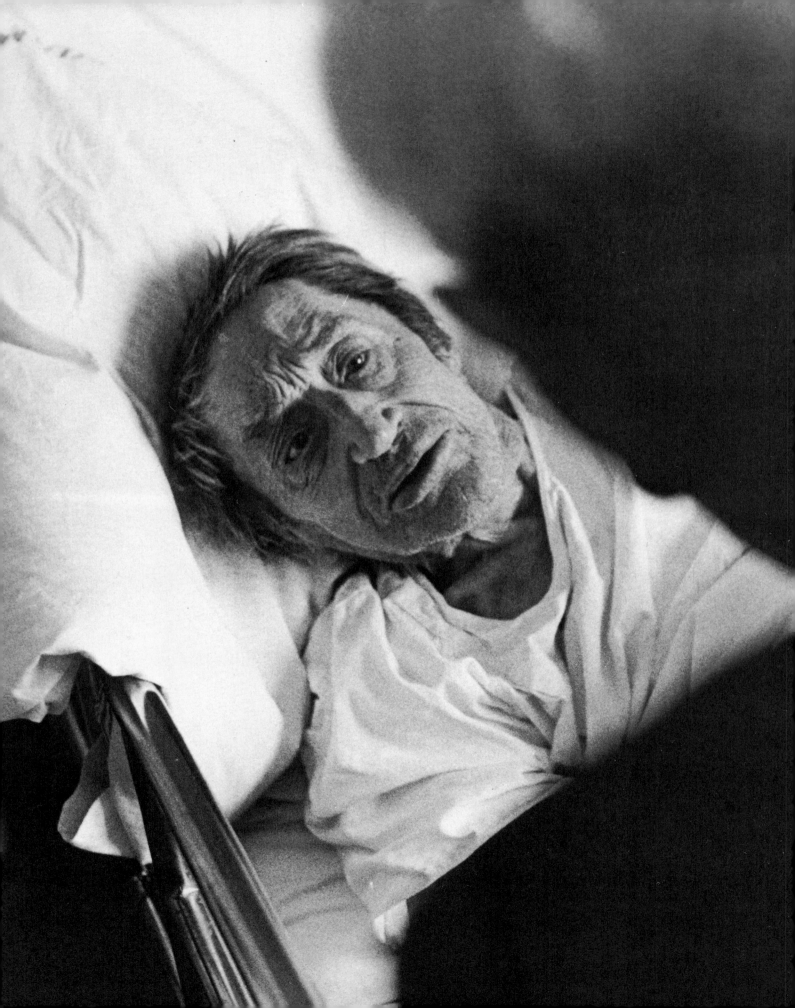

God gives us no more than we can bear, and
He gives patience first.

From frowning saints, good Lord, deliver us!

Rain from Heaven often comes when the gardener is least expecting it.

38

You must know that there is a time for par-
tridge and a time for penance.

What a torment for a poor soul that has attained this degree of union, to have to begin to deal with men again, to be condemned to see the miserable farce of life acted out before its eyes.

39

Strive like strong men until you die in the attempt, for you are here for nothing else than to strive.

All is nothing, except pleasing God.

I know not how I am so loved.

ST. TERESA OF AVILA

Teresa de (Cepeda y) Ahumada was born in Avila on March 28, 1515. After the death of her mother, when Teresa was twelve, she began—as she says in her autobiography—to go about with cousins who were slightly older and aroused "a desire for the world" in her. Her father responded by sending her to an Augustinian convent as a boarder, where she remained for eighteen months. In 1536 she entered the Carmelite Convent of the Incarnation in Avila as a novice. She was professed a year later.

It was in about 1555 that Teresa first began to think she was "sometimes being addressed by interior voices and to see certain visions and experience revelations." Following a vision of hell, she decided that the first thing she "could do for God . . . was to follow the vocation for a religious life which His Majesty had given me by keeping my Rule with the greatest possible perfection." It was this desire to observe the Rule of the Carmelite order "in its primitive rigor" that eventually led to the foundation of the Convent of St. Joseph in Avila.

At about the same time, Teresa was commanded by her superiors to write an account of her life, an autobiography that remains one of the world's great spiritual classics. Not long after, also on instructions from her superiors, she began the *Way of Perfection,* much of which was written at the height of the controversy over the reforms she was bringing about in the Carmelite order.

The Reform and the foundation of numerous Discalced Carmelite convents—at one of which she obtained the services of that other great Spanish mystic of the time, St. John of the Cross, as confessor—evoked the displeasure of the Carmelites of the Mitigated Observance and, in 1575, the General Chapter of the order passed sentence against the Discalced. Teresa was advised by her superiors to go to the convent at Toledo and there wrote what is widely regarded as her greatest work, the *Interior Castle,* a masterpiece of mystical literature.

In 1580 the Reformed Carmelites were made a separate Province and Teresa resumed her foundations and, in the year of her death, 1582, completed the *Foundations.* She died in Alba de Tormes on October 4. Teresa of Avila was beatified in 1614 and canonized in 1622.